THE GOLD COLOURING BOOK

THE GOLD COLOURING BOOK

BEAUTIFUL RADIANT DESIGNS

ARCTURUS

ARCTURUS
This edition published in 2016 by Arcturus Publishing Limited
26/27 Bickels Yard, 151–153 Bermondsey Street,
London SE1 3HA

978-1-78428-365-0
CH005377NT
Supplier 29, Date 0816, Print run 5495

Printed in China

Created for children 10+

This sumptuous colouring book based around the theme of gold is decorated throughout to celebrate the beauty of this precious metal. Many of the images in these pages are reminiscent of ancient arts, such as mosaics, decorative tiling and stained glass making. Each one has a small amount of gold detailing already added to give the picture a luxurious touch. You can either shade the images in jewel colours or in complementary metallic tones – just follow your instinct and you will be amazed at the results. So kick back, relax and get ready to enjoy a treasure trove of colouring riches!

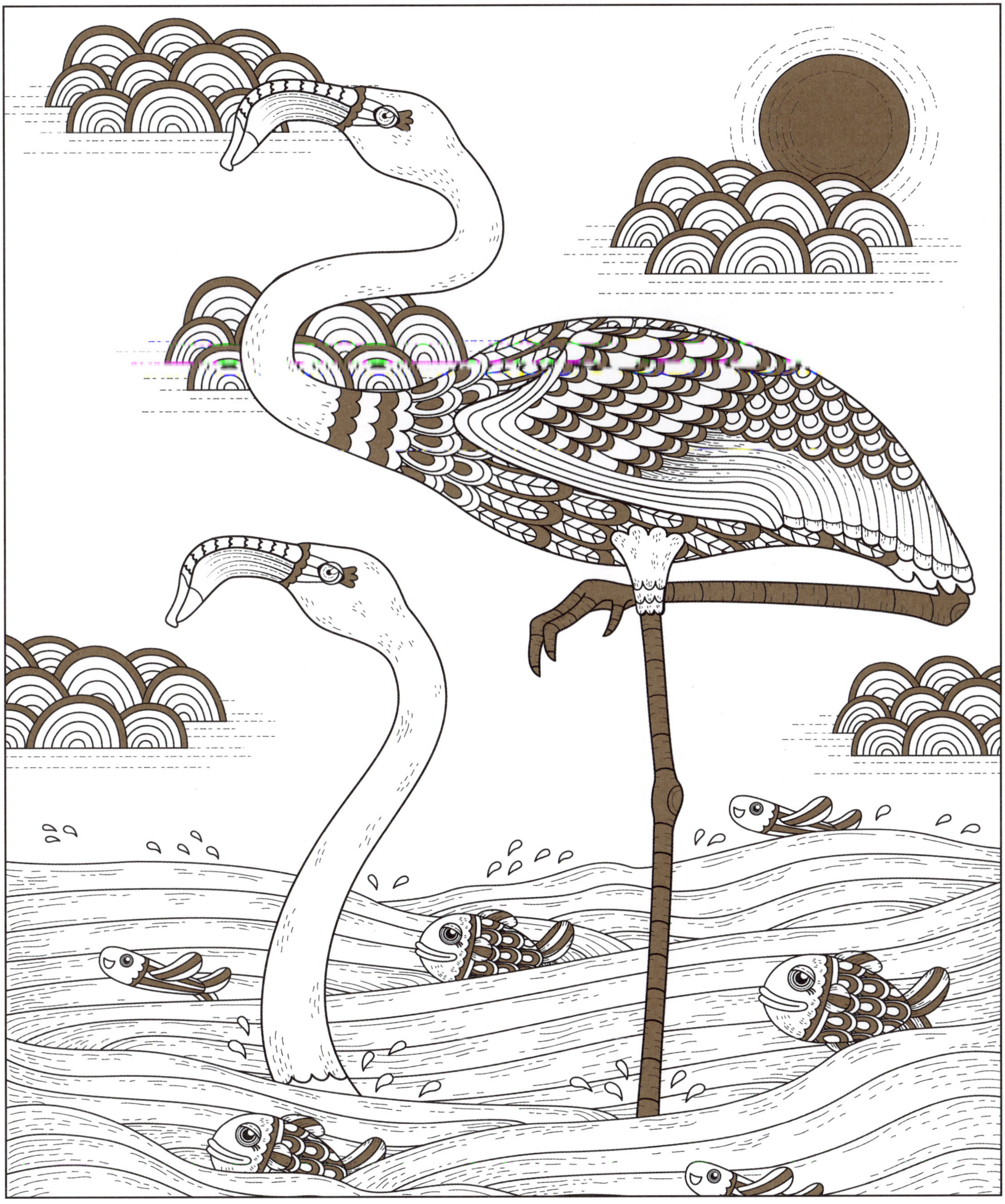

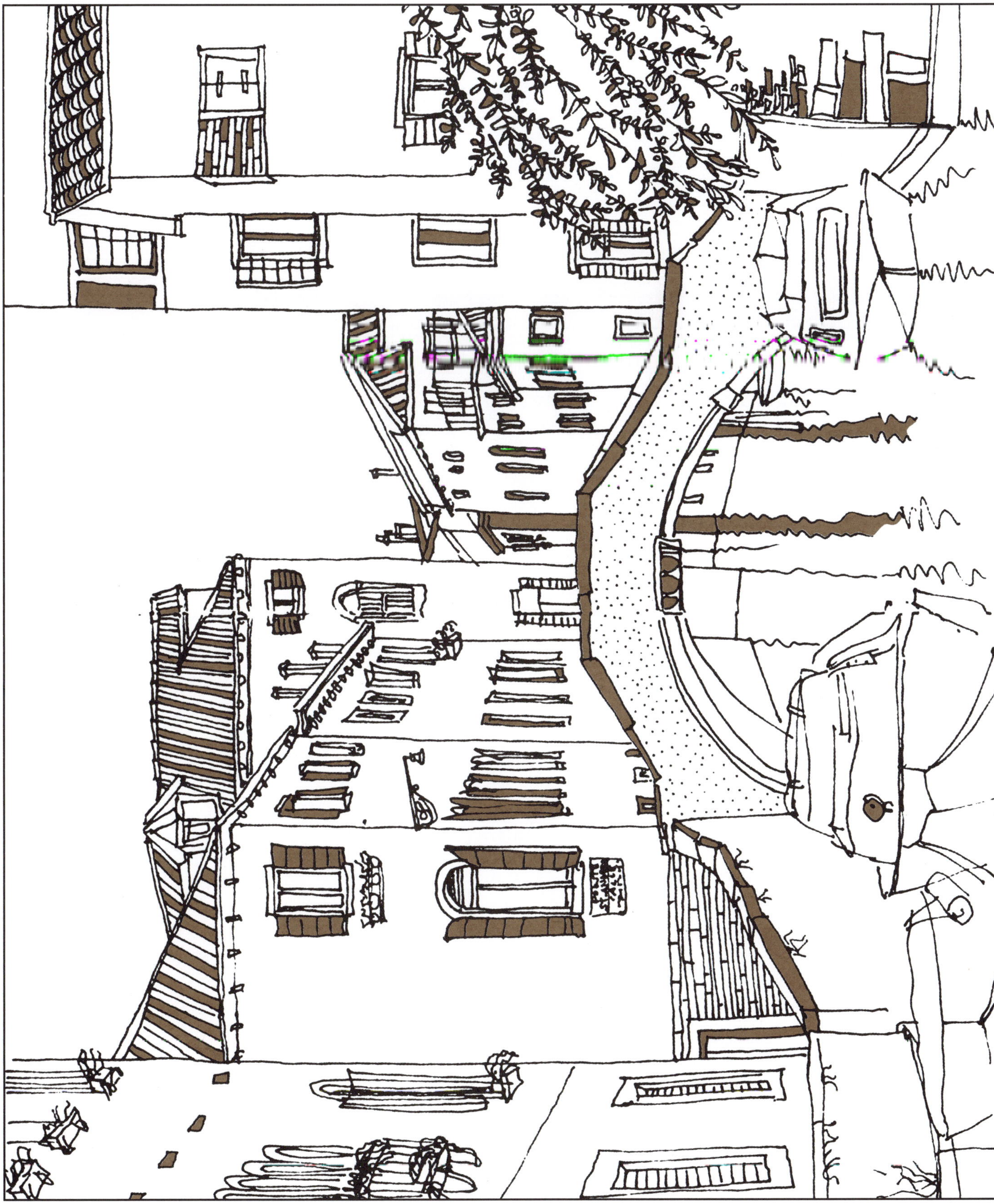

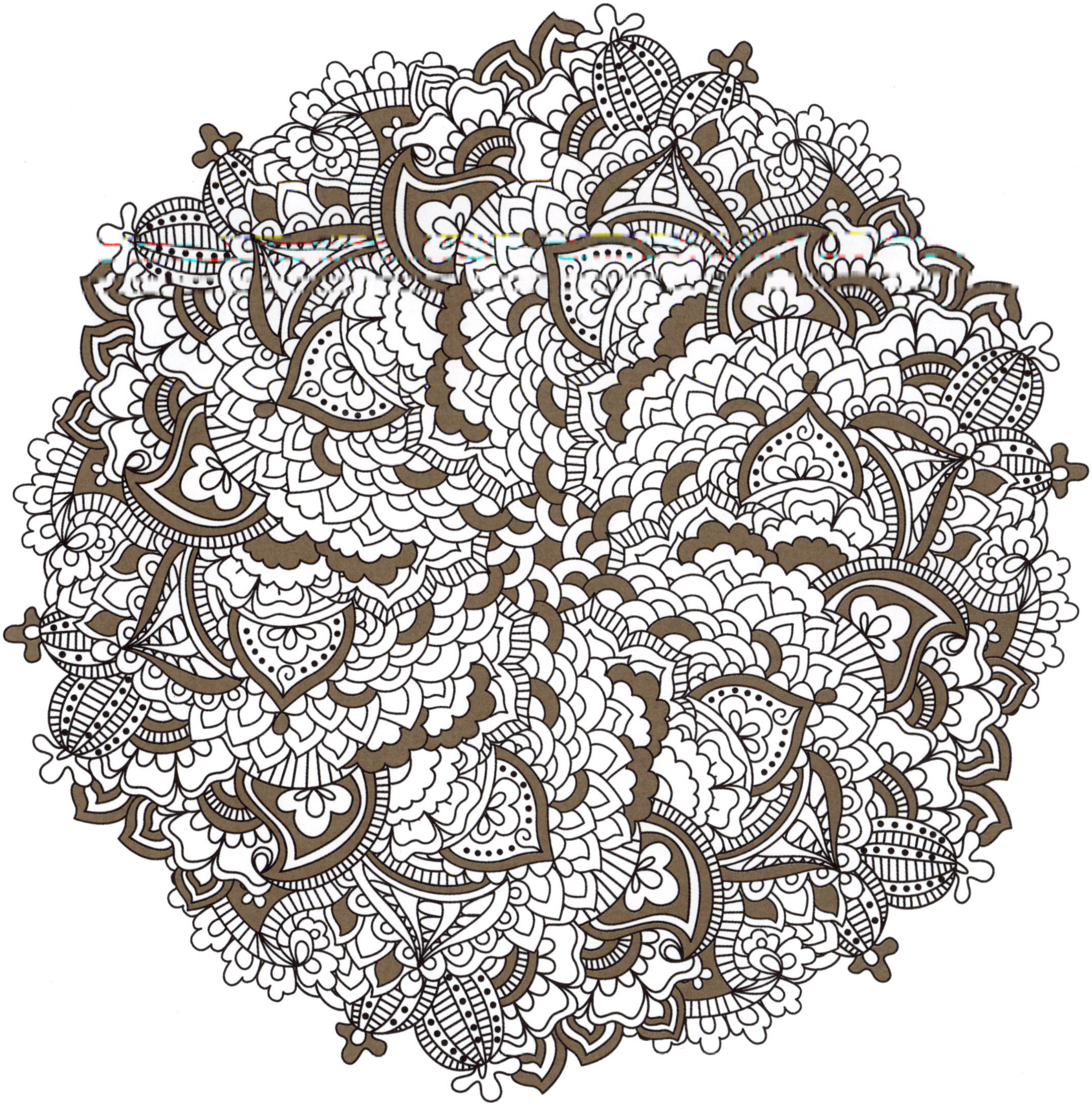